Breaking Barriers While Building Wealth:
A Guide to Financial Freedom for the Financial Diva
By Catrese Kilgore

Contents

Prelude

As I write this prelude, I'm filled with a sense of gratitude and excitement. This book is the culmination of a lifelong journey—a journey marked by bold choices, fierce determination, and the unwavering belief that financial empowerment is within reach for all of us.

My path to financial success has been a winding one, complete with both triumphs and stumbles. I've walked through the bustling streets of Wall Street and built my financial empire, not just through stocks and real estate, but through hard work, resilience, and a passion for learning.

I am not just an author; I am a Certified Public Accountant (CPA) with an investment portfolio that spans stocks, private equity, real estate, life insurance, and a mosaic of businesses. I am also a storyteller, eager to share the tapestry of experiences, trials, and triumphs that have shaped my path.

Throughout my career as a CPA, I have audited financial statements, prepared tax returns, and helped individuals and businesses navigate the complex landscape of numbers. But my journey is not limited to the confines of an office. It has taken me beyond the ledgers and into the exhilarating world of investments, where I've witnessed the power of compound interest and weathered market storms.

My real estate ventures have been akin to building a house from the ground up—brick by brick, just like the wealth I've accumulated. My passion for life insurance stems from the belief that it's not just about safeguarding against the uncertainties of life, but also about building a financial fortress for the future.

Owning and managing multiple businesses has been both exhilarating and challenging, akin to a thrilling rollercoaster ride. It has taught me valuable lessons in entrepreneurship, financial resilience, and the importance of adaptability.

Now, in the pages of this book, I want to share these experiences with you. I want to take you on a journey through the world of finance, demystifying complex concepts, and imparting practical wisdom. I want you to understand that financial empowerment is not a distant dream—it's a tangible reality within your grasp.

This book is not a magic formula for instant wealth, nor is it a promise of overnight success. It is a roadmap, a guide, and a mentor in your pursuit of financial confidence and independence. It is an invitation to embark on a journey of discovery, where you'll find not just knowledge but also inspiration, humor, and the reassurance that you are not alone on this path.

In these pages, I want to take you on a journey through my experiences and insights. I want to share the laughter and the tears, the moments of clarity and the times I've questioned my decisions. I want to inspire you to embrace your inner financial diva, to embark on your unique journey towards financial empowerment, and to believe in the possibilities that lie ahead.

This book is not about one-size-fits-all advice or get-rich-quick schemes. It's about finding your financial style, making informed decisions, and unleashing the sassy investor within you. It's about understanding that financial empowerment is not reserved for a select few—it's a path that anyone can tread with determination, knowledge, and a dash of style.

As you turn the pages remember that you're not alone on this journey. I'm right here with you, sharing my stories, insights, and humor. Remember that my words are not those of a distant expert but a fellow traveler. We will navigate the twists and turns of the financial landscape, armed with wisdom, resilience, and the confidence that comes from knowledge. Together, we'll explore the world of stocks, real estate, life insurance, and entrepreneurship, all while embracing the sassy, confident, and resilient financial diva within us.

May your financial journey be as empowering and fabulous as you've always dreamed,

Catrese Kilgore

Chapter 1: Unleashing the Stock Market Diva Within

Welcome to the exciting world of financial divas, where breaking barriers and building wealth is not just a dream but a reality waiting to be embraced. In this chapter, we'll demystify the stock market and delve into the intriguing universe of stocks, options, futures, and derivatives. It's like going on a glamorous shopping spree, but instead of fashion boutiques, you'll be navigating the financial markets with confidence, sass, and style. In the dazzling world of finance, I'm your guide, your guru, your stock market diva, and I'm here to reveal the glamorous secrets of making money in stocks. So, grab your favorite sparkly dress, put on those killer heels, and let's embark on a journey that's more fabulous than a designer handbag sale at the end of Fashion Week!

Demystifying the Stock Market: Where Glamour Meets Opportunity

Now, I know what you're thinking. The stock market can be as intimidating as a room full of snooty fashionistas sizing up your outfit. But fear not, my dear readers! I've been there, done that, and I'm here to tell you it's not all that complicated. Think of the stock market as your favorite boutique. You stroll in with cash (or a credit card), you pick out what you like, and voilà! You're an investor. No need for fancy degrees or a Wall Street address.

The beauty of it is that you don't need to be a financial wizard to get started. Just like picking out the perfect pair of sunglasses, you can learn to spot the right investments that suit your style.

The stock market, often portrayed as a realm reserved for Wall Street elites, is your playground for financial empowerment. It's not as intimidating as it may seem; think of it as your favorite high-end boutique, stocked with fabulous investment opportunities.

In today's digital age, investing in stocks is more accessible than ever, thanks to online platforms. These platforms are like your go-to online boutiques, where you can browse, research, and make investments from the comfort of your home.

Popular online brokerage platforms, such as E*TRADE, Robinhood, and Charles Schwab, offer a range of tools and resources to assist you in your stock investing journey. You can research companies, access real-time market data, and execute trades with just a few clicks. It's like having a personal shopper for your financial wardrobe, making the process of investing both convenient and efficient.

Online Chat Groups for Stock Investing: Your Stylish Support Network

In addition to online platforms, there's a wealth of knowledge and camaraderie to be found in online chat groups and forums dedicated to stock investing. These communities are your virtual fashion shows, where you can connect with fellow investors, share insights, and gain valuable tips.

Platforms like Reddit's r/Stocks, Stocktwits, and various Facebook groups provide spaces where you can discuss investment strategies, seek advice, and stay updated on market trends. Think of them as your backstage pass to the world of stock investing, where you can exchange ideas and experiences with like-minded individuals.

In my opinion, the easiest and least risky way to start your own stock portfolio is to open a Robinhood account. I opened my account in as little as five minutes using my Iphone. I filled out a simple questionnaire and within a day I had my own brokerage account waiting for my first deposit. I deposited $200, and bought my very first stock.

Stocks, also known as equities, are shares of ownership in a company. When you buy a stock, you become a shareholder and gain a stake in the company's success. It's like investing in a luxury handbag brand; as the brand's value grows, so does your investment.

But it's not just about owning shares; it's about the potential for both dividends and capital gains.

Dividend Stocks: Your Reliable Income Stream

Dividend stocks are like owning a collection of timeless fashion pieces that pay you dividends regularly. When you invest in dividend-paying companies, they share their profits with you as dividends. It's like having a reliable source of income that flows into your financial wardrobe season after season.

For example, think of dividend stocks as your favorite designer handbags. Not only do they appreciate in value over time, but they also pay you dividends, much like receiving compliments and admiration every time you carry your prized handbag.

Capital Gains Benefits: Fashionable Profits

Now, let's talk about capital gains—the stylish profits you can make when the value of your investments increases. Just as a fashion-forward trendsetter buys unique pieces and watches their value rise, investing in stocks can lead to capital gains when the stock price appreciates.

Capital gains can be short-term or long-term. Short-term gains apply to investments held for less than a year and are typically taxed at a higher rate. Long-term gains, on the other hand, apply to investments held for over a year and often come with more favorable tax rates. It's like making an investment in a trendy accessory and watching it become a collector's item over time.

Exploring Financial Instruments: Beyond Stocks

Options are like custom-tailored financial contracts. They give you the right (but not the obligation) to buy or sell a stock at a specific price within a set timeframe. It's akin to having the option to purchase that designer dress you've had your eye on at a fixed price, regardless of market fluctuations.

Futures contracts are commitments to buy or sell an asset at a predetermined price and date in the future. Think of them as advance orders for a limited-edition fashion item; you lock in the price today, ensuring you get it when it's released.

Derivatives are financial instruments that derive their value from an underlying asset, such as stocks, bonds, or commodities. They can be used for risk management or speculation. It's like accessorizing your investment portfolio with unique pieces that enhance its value and flexibility.

Understanding these financial instruments empowers you to make informed investment choices. They're not just tools for financial professionals; they're your accessories for building wealth.

The Power of Compound Interest: Buy and Hold!

Ladies and gentlemen, let me introduce you to the unsung hero of wealth building: compound interest. It's like stumbling upon a designer dress that's been marked down to a fraction of its original price, and you know it's going to appreciate over time. When you invest wisely and let your money grow, it's like having an ever-expanding wardrobe that never goes out of style.

Now, I don't know about you, but I'd much rather have my money work for me than the other way around. That's the magic of compound interest. You set it and forget it, just like that fabulous dress you bought on sale. It keeps appreciating, and you look like a financial fashionista without even trying!

Imagine you've found a fabulous dress on sale, and you decide to buy it. You wear it to a glamorous event, and everyone admires it. But what if I told you that your investment in stocks can be just as rewarding?

Compound interest is the magic behind long-term investing. It's the snowball effect of earning returns on your initial investment, plus the returns on your returns. Over time, your money can grow exponentially, much like investing in a timeless fashion piece that appreciates in value.

By holding onto your investments and reinvesting your earnings, you harness the power of compound interest. It's not a get-rich-quick scheme; it's a strategy that, over time, can transform small investments into substantial wealth. So, embrace the buy-and-hold approach and watch your financial wardrobe flourish.

Finding Your Investing Style: Risk-Taking Fashionista or Conservative Trendsetter?

Investing is a lot like fashion; it's all about your unique style. Some people prefer to take risks and go for the latest trends, just like those daring fashionistas who don avant-garde outfits that turn heads. Others like to play it safe, sticking to classic pieces that never go out of style, much like the conservative trendsetters who rock timeless elegance.

Finding your investing style is essential. Are you the kind of person who gets a thrill from the latest tech gadgets, or do you prefer the reliability of a little black dress that always looks good? I'll help you figure that out because, let's face it, not everyone can pull off those high-risk investments like they're runway models.

Just as fashionistas have distinct styles—some daring and avant-garde, others classic and timeless—investors also have unique preferences. Are you a risk-taking fashionista, eager to explore high-risk, high-reward investments, or a conservative trendsetter, prioritizing stability and slow but steady growth?

Your investing style should align with your financial goals, risk tolerance, and time horizon. It's about choosing the investment "outfit" that suits you best and complements your financial journey.

How to Research and Choose Stocks: Curating a Fabulous Wardrobe of Investments

Now, let's talk about the fun part: curating your investment portfolio, aka your financial wardrobe. Just like shopping for the perfect outfit, researching and choosing stocks can be an exhilarating adventure.

You want to look for stocks that align with your style and goals. Do you go for flashy, high-growth companies, or do you prefer established, dividend-paying stocks that provide a steady income? It's like deciding between a sequined evening gown for a night on the town or a comfy pair of jeans for a laid-back weekend.

But remember, my fellow divas, it's not just about the looks. We need substance too. So, I'll teach you how to dive into financial statements and analyze a company's fundamentals. It's like checking the fabric and stitching of a garment to make sure it's top-notch quality. Researching and selecting stocks is akin to curating a fabulous wardrobe. It's about making informed choices that reflect your style and preferences.

Start by studying the companies you're interested in. Understand their financial health, growth potential, and competitive advantages. It's like examining the craftsmanship and quality of a fashion piece before making a purchase.

Diversify your investments, just as you'd diversify your wardrobe. Don't put all your money into a single stock; spread it across different sectors and industries to minimize risk. Think of it as having a versatile wardrobe that's ready for any occasion.

As you venture deeper into the world of finance, remember that becoming a Stock Market Diva is not just about making money—it's about gaining the knowledge, confidence, and style to navigate this exciting terrain. So, embrace your inner diva, invest wisely, and let your financial journey be as glamorous and empowering as you deserve!

Chapter 2: Building Your Empire Brick by Brick

Welcome to the fabulous world of real estate, where the path to prosperity is paved with bricks, style, and savvy investments. In this chapter, we'll dive into the art of rental property, the significance of location, financing strategies, the allure of Real Estate Investment Trusts (REITs), and the exciting world of Airbnb-style investments. Think of it as discovering the trendiest fashion district, only this time, it's about properties, potential, and profit.

The Art of Rental Property: Think of Tenants as Your Loyal Clientele, and Maintenance as a Fabulous Makeover!

Investing in rental properties allows you to step into the role of the ultimate diva—your tenants' happiness is your ultimate goal, and the properties themselves are your canvas. Picture this: you're the director of a show, and each unit is a character in your story. From selecting the right paint color to ensuring the faucets don't drip, it's about creating living spaces that tenants adore.

Remember, real estate investing isn't just about owning properties; it's about providing exceptional living experiences for your tenants while steadily growing your wealth. Be the diva landlord who adds style and substance to your real estate portfolio.

Let's dive deeper into the realm of rental properties. Imagine yourself as the landlord of a luxurious rental property, and your tenants are your loyal clientele. The property itself is your personal fashion canvas, and its maintenance is akin to giving it a fabulous makeover!

Much like a fashionista carefully curates her collection, you must choose your tenants wisely. Background checks, ironclad rental agreements, and crystal-clear communication are your tools to ensure your property remains in tip-top shape. It's all about finding that perfect balance between style and substance.

Remember, maintaining your property is like having a fashion emergency kit. A leaking faucet becomes the equivalent of a stain on a silk blouse; it demands immediate attention! But with a little TLC and some strategic investments, your real estate empire will be runway-ready in no time.

Renovations and upgrades can transform a mediocre property into a showstopper, just like a fabulous pair of shoes can elevate any outfit. But be cautious, my friend! Renovations can quickly become a money pit if you're not careful. Just like those designer shoes that end up hurting your feet, unexpected costs can wreak havoc on your budget. Plan wisely, get multiple quotes, and keep an eye on the return on investment (ROI) before embarking on a renovation spree.

Now, let's talk about property management, shall we? It's like having a personal stylist for your real estate investments. Being a landlord can be rewarding, but it also comes with its fair share of challenges. It's like wearing high heels all day - glamorous, but sometimes uncomfortable. From finding tenants to handling repairs and maintenance, managing properties requires organization and a touch of patience. But fear not, you can always hire a property management company to handle the nitty-gritty details while you focus on expanding your real estate empire. Whether you choose to manage your properties yourself or hire a professional, this decision should align with your personal style and preferences. It's like deciding between DIY fashion fixes and seeking the advice of a professional tailor to create that perfect fit.

Location, Location, Location: Discovering the Hottest Fashion District!

In real estate, location isn't just everything—it's the fashion district where trends are set and fortunes are made. Selecting the right neighborhood is akin to discovering that exclusive address where style, convenience, and potential converge.

I once invested in a neighborhood undergoing a remarkable transformation. It had character but was undervalued. As the area evolved into a vibrant hub with trendy boutiques and dining establishments, my property's value skyrocketed. It was like being a fashion trendsetter ahead of the curve, but in the realm of real estate. The lesson here is clear: diligent neighborhood research and an eye for trends can make a significant difference in your real estate success. Just as fashionistas scout the hottest districts for the latest trends, real estate investors hunt for promising locations to build their wealth.

So, how do you find the perfect neighborhood? Research, my dear divas! Investigate the area's growth potential, school districts, local amenities, and crime rates. Think of it as scouting for the latest fashion trends; you want to be ahead of the curve.

And don't forget to consider your personal style. Are you a city slicker or a suburban fashionista? Your investment should reflect your lifestyle, much like your wardrobe does.

Furthermore, the neighborhood's long-term potential is crucial. Think of it as investing in a timeless piece of clothing, something that never goes out of style. You want your property to appreciate over time, just like a classic designer handbag that only gets more valuable with age.

Financing Tricks: Get the Best Mortgage Rates!

Now, let's talk about the power of leverage. Just like when you wear high heels and instantly feel taller, leverage allows you to amplify your returns. By using other people's money (OPM), such as a mortgage, you can control a more significant investment with less of your own capital. It's like strutting around in designer shoes without paying the full price upfront. But remember, just like walking in heels, leverage can be risky if not managed properly. So, make sure to evaluate the potential risks and rewards before taking the plunge.

Securing financing for your real estate ventures is like finding those coveted luxury shoes you've been eyeing at a steep discount. It's a game-changer. You want to negotiate like a pro, comparing rates and terms as if you're haggling at a designer sample sale. Mortgage rates can significantly impact your investment returns.

Here's a personal tip that has proven invaluable: maintain excellent credit. Having a good credit score is your fashion statement. It opens doors and gets you exclusive deals. Just as a fashionista takes impeccable care of her wardrobe, ensure your credit score is in top shape. This will help you qualify for lower interest rates, saving you a substantial amount over the life of your mortgage.

Moreover, don't settle for the first mortgage offer that comes your way. Just as you would explore different stores for the perfect pair of shoes, shop around among various lenders to find the mortgage terms that best suit your needs. This diligent approach can yield substantial savings and boost your investment's profitability. Paying attention to interest rates, loan types, and down payment options is like choosing between high heels and flats—each has its place in your financial wardrobe.

Remember, my fellow investors, the goal is to look fabulous without breaking the bank. So, shop around for those financing deals, just like you'd scour every corner of the store during a shoe sale, and strut your stuff in the world of real estate.

Alternative Investments: Vacation Rentals to REITs, Diversify Like a Fashion-Forward Trendsetter!

Fashionistas don't limit themselves to just one style, and neither should your investments! Diversification is the name of the game. Just like mixing and matching clothing pieces to create stunning outfits, you can explore alternative real estate investments to diversify your portfolio.

Let's shift our focus to a captivating real estate investment avenue: Real Estate Investment Trusts, or REITs. Think of REITs as your chance to diversify your real estate portfolio without the responsibilities of property management.

REITs are akin to owning a curated collection of high-end fashion brands in your investment portfolio. They allow you to invest in a range of real estate assets—ranging from residential properties to commercial buildings—without the burden of owning and managing individual properties. It's like enjoying the benefits of real estate ownership without the hands-on work.

Imagine owning shares in a REIT that specializes in luxury hotels. As the hospitality industry thrives, so do your returns. It's like savoring the profits from a high-end fashion brand without the need for a physical boutique.

Remember that REITs offer liquidity, diversification, and the potential for regular income through dividends. Just as a fashion-forward trendsetter diversifies her wardrobe, consider incorporating REITs into your real estate investment strategy to enhance your portfolio's flexibility and potential for growth.

Diversifying your real estate empire not only spreads risk but also adds a layer of excitement to your financial journey. So, be that trendsetter who experiments with different styles, and watch your empire flourish.

Airbnb-Style Investments: Ride the Wave of Short-Term Rentals

Now, let's explore the thrilling world of Airbnb-style investments. Picture this: you have a property, whether it's a cozy apartment or a charming cottage, and you're turning it into a short-term rental. It's like running your own boutique hotel, complete with personalized experiences for your guests.

The rise of platforms like Airbnb has transformed the way people travel, providing unique alternatives to traditional hotels. Investing in short-term rentals can be highly profitable, with the potential for higher rental income compared to long-term leases.

However, it's crucial to be mindful of local regulations, property management, and maintaining the property's appeal to guests. Short-term rentals require a different approach compared to traditional leasing, but with the right strategy, they can be a lucrative addition to your real estate portfolio.

In conclusion, dear real estate aficionados, building your empire one brick at a time is not merely a financial journey—it's a glamorous adventure filled with opportunities, personal anecdotes, and a sense of style. Whether you're revamping rental properties, scouting promising neighborhoods, securing financing, exploring REITs, or venturing into Airbnb-style investments, let your inner diva shine. Real estate is your stage, and your empire awaits its grand unveiling, one stylish property at a time.

Chapter 3: Life Insurance and Beyond: Protecting Our Glamorous Legacy

Welcome back, my fellow financial fashionistas, to our captivating journey towards financial empowerment! We're diving headfirst into the world of life insurance, where we'll learn how to protect our fabulous legacies and ensure that our financial empire remains as radiant as ever. We will explore the nuances between term life insurance and whole life insurance. Plus, we'll shine a spotlight on disability insurance—an essential component of securing our glamorous legacies.

Life Insurance Essentials: Wearing a Fabulous Red Lipstick That Never Fades!

Think of life insurance as that timeless, bold red lipstick that never fades, always making a statement. It's a financial accessory that adds a touch of glamour to your portfolio. Life insurance provides a safety net, ensuring that your loved ones are financially secure, just like that perfect red shade accentuates your smile.

Now, the essentials of life insurance can be as simple as picking the right shade of red. Term life insurance offers straightforward protection for a specific period, while permanent life insurance, like whole or universal life, is more like a long-lasting, rich lip color. It's an investment in your future, and it never goes out of style.

Before we dive into the details, let's revisit the essence of life insurance. Life insurance is the financial accessory that adds a touch of glamour to your portfolio, ensuring that your loved ones remain financially secure, much like that perfect red shade accentuates your smile.

How to Select the Right Life Insurance Policy

Selecting the right life insurance policy is akin to dressing for a glamorous event. You wouldn't wear casual attire to a black-tie affair, right? Similarly, your life insurance policy should be tailored to your unique needs and goals.

There are two primary types of life insurance: term and whole life. Term insurance is like renting a designer gown for a specific occasion—it provides coverage for a set period. Whole life insurance, on the other hand, is like investing in a custom-made couture dress—it offers lifelong coverage and builds cash value over time.

Consider your financial situation, long-term goals, and the needs of your loved ones when choosing the right policy. It's all about finding the perfect "outfit" for your financial wardrobe.

Decoding the Jargon: Cash Value, Dividends, and Other Mysterious Terms

Life insurance can be filled with jargon that sounds as mysterious as a haute couture fashion show. But fret not; we're here to decode the terms:

- Cash Value
  - Think of cash value as the equity in your life insurance policy.
  - It's like the hidden treasures you discover in the pockets of your favorite coat.
  - Over time, your policy accumulates cash value, which you can access or use to pay premiums.
- Dividends
  - Just like when a fashion house shares its profits with shareholders, some life insurance policies pay dividends to policyholders.
  - Can be reinvested or used as income.
  - It's like receiving a special bonus from your policy.
- Term
  - Term refers to the length of coverage in term life insurance.
  - It's like renting a designer dress for a specific event—it's only in effect for a set period.

Understanding these terms allows you to make informed decisions and ensures you're speaking the language of financial divas.

Tips for Selecting the Right Insurer and Policy

When it comes to selecting the right insurer and policy, think of it as finding your personal stylist. You want someone who understands your unique style and needs.

Here are some tips:

- Research
  - Just as you'd research a fashion designer before purchasing their creations, research insurance companies.
  - Look for reputable insurers with a strong track record.

- Compare Quotes
  - Get quotes from multiple insurers to find the best deal.
  - It's like trying on different outfits to find the one that fits perfectly.

- Assess Your Needs
  - Consider your financial situation, your loved ones' needs, and your long-term goals.
  - This helps you determine the type and amount of coverage you require.

- Ask Questions
  - Don't be shy about asking questions. Whether it's about premiums, riders, or policy details, seek clarification. It's like getting fashion advice from a trusted stylist.

- Review Regularly
  - Just as you'd update your wardrobe to stay fashionable, regularly review your life insurance policy to ensure it still aligns with your financial goals.

Term Life Insurance: A Fashionable Choice for Protection

Term life insurance is your go-to for straightforward, cost-effective protection. It's the little black dress of the insurance world—simple, elegant, and always in style. Just like you'd choose the perfect LBD for a classic look, term life insurance is ideal for those seeking temporary coverage during specific life stages.

With term life, you select a coverage period (the "term")—typically 10, 20, or 30 years. If you pass away during this term, your beneficiaries receive the death benefit, tax-free. It's like buying an exquisite designer outfit for a specific occasion, ensuring you look your best without breaking the bank.

One of the significant advantages of term life insurance is its affordability. You pay premiums, and in return, your loved ones are protected in case of your untimely departure. It's a no-frills, essential piece of your financial wardrobe.

Whole Life Insurance: The Couture Choice for Lifelong Protection

Now, let's talk about whole life insurance—the couture choice for lifelong protection. Whole life insurance is like that bespoke, handcrafted gown designed to fit you perfectly. It provides coverage for your entire life, and its unique feature is the cash value component that accumulates over time.

Think of the cash value as the equivalent of investing in a collection of luxurious designer handbags. With whole life insurance, a portion of your premium payments is set aside to grow tax-deferred. You can access this cash value during your lifetime for various financial needs, such as paying for college, funding a dream vacation, or supplementing your retirement income.

Whole life insurance also guarantees a death benefit to your beneficiaries, regardless of when you pass away. It's the financial equivalent of having a timeless, iconic piece in your wardrobe that never goes out of style.

Disability Insurance: Safeguarding Your Financial Chic

Now, let's not forget disability insurance—a must-have in your financial wardrobe. Disability insurance is like that reliable and versatile blazer that pairs perfectly with any outfit. It protects your income in case you become unable to work due to illness or injury.

Much like life insurance, disability insurance is available in two main forms: short-term and long-term. Short-term disability provides coverage for a limited duration, usually a few months to a year, while long-term disability insurance kicks in when a disability lasts for an extended period.

Disability insurance ensures that even if life throws you a curveball, your financial chic remains intact. It provides you with a source of income to maintain your lifestyle, cover essential expenses, and keep the fashion-forward vibe going.

The Importance of Beneficiaries: Who Will Inherit Your Fabulous Empire?

When it comes to life insurance, choosing your beneficiaries is crucial. Think of them as the rightful heirs to your glamorous empire. You want to ensure that the fruits of your financial labor go to the right hands, just like you'd pass down your most cherished heirloom jewelry to a deserving loved one.

Selecting beneficiaries requires careful consideration. It's not just about who you love; it's also about who depends on you financially. Are you providing for your children, a partner, or even a beloved charity? The choice is yours, but it's essential to ensure your financial legacy is passed down as intended.

Creative Insurance Strategies: Leave a Legacy Worthy of a Glamorous Hollywood Starlet!

Life insurance isn't just about protection; it's also a strategic tool for building a legacy worthy of a glamorous Hollywood starlet. Creative insurance strategies can help you grow your wealth, just like clever fashion choices can elevate your style game.

Consider using policies like indexed universal life insurance or variable universal life insurance to accumulate cash value that can be invested. It's like having a secret vault of fabulous outfits that appreciate in value over time. These policies can be used for supplemental retirement income, funding your child's education, or even as a source of emergency funds.

Estate Planning: Like Organizing Your Wardrobe, Plan Your Assets for Maximum Impact!

Estate planning is the final touch on your financial ensemble, much like organizing your wardrobe for maximum impact. It's about ensuring that your assets are distributed according to your wishes efficiently and with minimal tax impact.

Just as you'd carefully select the right accessories to complement your outfit, estate planning allows you to choose the right legal instruments to preserve your wealth. Consider tools like trusts, wills, and power of attorney to ensure a seamless transition of your financial empire to your heirs. It's like having a trusted stylist who knows your style preferences inside and out.

And don't forget about tax implications. A well-thought-out estate plan can help minimize the tax burden on your heirs, leaving more of your hard-earned assets in their hands, where they belong.

So, my glamorous readers, as we conclude Chapter 3, remember that life insurance and disability insurance are not mere financial accessories; they're essential pieces of your legacy puzzle. Whether you choose term or whole life insurance, and add disability insurance to your collection, you're securing a legacy that's as enduring and fabulous as you are. Life insurance is not just a financial safety net; it's a key element in protecting and growing your fabulous legacy. Just like you'd carefully curate your wardrobe to reflect your style and personality, life insurance allows you to design a financial legacy that exudes your unique charm and sophistication.

Chapter 4: Balancing Act: Multiple Businesses for the Boss Lady

Today, we're stepping into the world of multiple businesses, where we'll discuss the art of managing diverse enterprises with the grace and flair of a true boss lady. In this chapter, we'll explore the profound significance of owning businesses as a means to pass on financial success to future generations. Unlike a regular job, businesses can become a lasting legacy that your children and their children can inherit and nurture.

Generational Wealth: Why a Regular Job Won't Cut It

Let's begin with a stark reality: a regular job is like a fleeting fashion trend—it comes and goes. But if we aspire to leave a financial legacy that endures for generations, we must think beyond the confines of traditional employment.

Passing down a 9-to-5 job to your child simply isn't feasible. Your position, your office, your paycheck— all tied to you. Once you retire or move on, that job typically vanishes, leaving your children without a sustainable source of income. It's like having a fabulous couture gown that can't be tailored to fit the next generation.

Business ownership, on the other hand, allows us to create something of lasting value. It's like establishing a fashion brand that continues to thrive, season after season, long after you've stepped off the runway. Let's delve deeper into the importance of generational wealth through business ownership.

The Legacy of Business Ownership: Passing the Torch

Owning a business is akin to creating an enduring legacy, one that can be passed from generation to generation. Just as a timeless fashion brand evolves and adapts, so too can your family's business, providing a consistent source of income for your descendants.

Imagine your child stepping into your well-established business, inheriting not just the assets but also the knowledge and experience you've amassed over the years. It's like handing them the designer blueprint for success, a roadmap that can guide them toward financial prosperity.

The secret to building generational wealth lies in nurturing and expanding your business while grooming your successors to take the helm. Just as a fashion house's creative director prepares the next generation of designers, your role is to equip your heirs with the skills and knowledge needed to sustain and grow the family enterprise.

Financial Growth Strategies: Cultivating Prosperity Like a Master Gardener

Expanding your family's business is akin to cultivating a flourishing garden. Just as a skilled gardener carefully tends to the soil, plants, and flowers, you must nurture your business endeavors to ensure they thrive.

Diversification is your gardening toolkit. Just as a variety of plants adds vibrancy and resilience to a garden, consider diversifying your business interests. Explore new markets, products, or services that complement your core enterprise. This creates a financial ecosystem that can weather economic changes and adapt to evolving consumer tastes.

Investing wisely is your soil conditioner. Just as a gardener enriches the soil for optimal growth, you should allocate resources strategically. Monitor cash flow, trim unnecessary expenses, and make informed investments that promote growth. A well-nurtured business is like a flourishing garden—bountiful and enduring.

The Hustle Mindset: From Lemonade Stands to Global Empires, We've Got This!

The hustle mindset is where it all begins. From those childhood lemonade stands to building global empires, it's a journey that mirrors the evolution of a fashionista's style—from experimenting with colors and patterns to finding one's signature look.

Just like we've refined our fashion sense over the years, growing multiple businesses requires adaptability and a willingness to learn. Embrace the entrepreneurial spirit and channel your inner go-getter. Remember, your financial empire is like a curated collection of your favorite fashion pieces, each venture contributing to your unique style.

Navigating the Business World: Walking the Red Carpet, with Fierce Determination!

Navigating the business world is akin to strutting down the red carpet, and you, my dear readers, are the star of the show. It's about showcasing your talent, determination, and unique style.

Much like a red carpet event, preparation is key. You need a strong business plan, a clear vision, and the ability to stand out from the crowd. Just as a fashionista knows how to make a statement with her outfit, you must differentiate your businesses and establish your brand's identity.

Networking is your VIP party invitation. Just as celebrities mingle with the who's who of Hollywood, you should connect with industry peers, mentors, and potential partners. Surrounding yourself with the right people is like selecting the perfect accessories to complement your ensemble—it elevates your overall look.

Financial Growth Strategies: Scale Your Business Like a Superstar Launching a New Fragrance Line!

Now, let's talk about financial growth strategies. Scaling your business is akin to a superstar launching a new fragrance line. It's all about creating buzz and expanding your presence in the market.

Diversification is your secret weapon. Just as a fashion brand expands from clothing to accessories and fragrances, consider diversifying your business portfolio. Explore new markets, products, or services that complement your existing ventures. It's like creating a full fashion ensemble, complete with accessories and signature scents.

Financial discipline is your red carpet glow. Just as stars maintain their radiance with skincare routines and beauty regimens, your businesses thrive when you manage finances wisely. Monitor cash flow, cut unnecessary expenses, and invest strategically. It's like maintaining your impeccable appearance for every public appearance.

Managing Multiple Ventures: Juggling Businesses Like a Pro, Without Dropping a Single Diamond!

Managing multiple ventures is the ultimate balancing act, much like juggling priceless diamonds without a single one dropping to the ground. It's about organization, delegation, and impeccable timing. As your family's financial maestro, managing multiple business ventures is like orchestrating a symphony of success. Each venture is an instrument, contributing its unique notes to create a harmonious and prosperous melody.

Create a harmonious ensemble of businesses. Just as a fashionista coordinates her outfits with precision, align your ventures to complement each other. Leverage synergies and shared resources whenever possible to maximize efficiency. Balancing multiple businesses requires finesse, much like a conductor coordinating a symphony. Ensure that your ventures align with your overall financial goals, leveraging synergies and shared resources where possible. This orchestration ensures efficiency and maximizes returns.

Delegate responsibilities like a true CEO. Delegation is your conductor's baton. Just as a conductor relies on skilled musicians to bring the music to life, you must assemble a talented reliable team to manage and nurture your various ventures. Delegate responsibilities to experts in their respective fields, allowing you to focus on strategic direction and overall orchestration.

And never underestimate the power of time management. Time management is your tempo control. Just as a celebrity juggles red carpet appearances and movie shoots, allocate your time wisely among your various ventures. Prioritize tasks, set clear goals, and be ready to adapt to changing circumstances and unforeseen challenges. CJ Tate's book, "Mastering the Clock: The Ultimate Guide to Time Management" is a quick read filled with useful tips in time management.

In conclusion, managing multiple businesses is a testament to your entrepreneurial prowess. Like curating a diverse wardrobe filled with stunning pieces, each business adds its unique flair to your financial empire. The journey to building generational wealth through business ownership is a testament to your dedication and foresight. Just as a fashion designer creates a timeless brand, each business venture contributes to the fabric of your family's financial legacy. Consider the importance of nurturing this legacy, diversifying your financial interests, and skillfully managing multiple ventures like a true visionary.

Remember you have the power to create a financial legacy that endures for generations to come. Much like the fashion icons who've left an indelible mark on the industry, your family's business endeavors can become a lasting testament to your financial acumen and entrepreneurial spirit.

Chapter 5: Savvy Strategies for Debt Management

Hello, my dazzling financial fashionistas, and welcome to the stylish world of debt management. Tackling debt can be as exhilarating as clearing out your closet. Think of it as decluttering your financial wardrobe to make room for new, glamorous additions.

Tackling Debt with Style: Clearing Out Your Closet to Make Room for Fabulous New Pieces!

Your debt is like those outdated, ill-fitting clothes lurking at the back of your closet. They're weighing you down, cramping your style, and it's high time for a fashion-forward makeover. Debt management is your ticket to a more fabulous, debt-free wardrobe!

Dealing with debt is a bit like revamping your closet—it requires a keen eye for what stays and what goes. Those high-interest debts hanging in your financial closet? They're the outdated, ill-fitting garments you can't wait to get rid of. Debt management is your chance to perform a dazzling wardrobe makeover on your finances.

Start by taking inventory of your debts. Just as you'd go through your closet, identifying the pieces that no longer serve your style, it's time to audit your debts. List out all your outstanding balances, from credit cards to loans. It's time to shine a spotlight on your financial fashion choices. Once you've got a clear picture, you can start streamlining your debt collection with the confidence of a top-tier stylist.

Prioritizing Debt Repayment: Pay Off High-Interest Debts Like Returning an Ill-Fitting Dress!

When it comes to debt repayment, prioritize high-interest debts just like you'd ditch that overpriced, ill-fitting dress that's been collecting dust in your wardrobe. These high-interest debts are the fashion faux pas of your financial portfolio, and it's time to bid them adieu!

Channel your inner Marie Kondo and declutter your debts in style. Identify those debts with the highest interest rates—they're the proverbial wardrobe rejects that need to go first. Allocate extra funds to pay them off first. Clearing out high-interest debts leaves your financial closet lighter. This is like donating the clothes you no longer need to make room for new, stylish additions to your wardrobe. By reducing high-interest debts, you're freeing up financial space for fabulous new opportunities.

Negotiating Lower Interest Rates: Channel Your Inner Negotiator and Save Money Like a Boss!

Remember those times you eyed a designer piece that was just a tad over your budget? What did you do? Negotiate, naturally! The same savvy approach applies to your debts. Channel your inner negotiator and haggle for lower interest rates with the finesse of a seasoned shopper.

Reach out to your creditors—it's like negotiating for that coveted fashion find. Just like you'd bargain for that statement handbag, ask if they can lower your interest rates. Explain your financial goals and how a rate reduction would benefit both sides. You'd be surprised how open they can be to accommodate your request.

And don't forget, every dollar saved on interest is a dollar you can invest in your fabulous future. Negotiating lower interest rates is like scoring a designer piece on sale—it's a triumph for your financial wardrobe!

Building Credit Like a Fashion Icon: Flaunt Your Credit Score Like a Fabulous Accessory!

Your credit score is your financial accessory, so why not flaunt it like a fashion icon? Just as you'd proudly display a statement necklace or a chic pair of sunglasses, your credit score should be showcased with the same panache.

Maintaining a dazzling credit score is a bit like perfecting your signature style. Pay your bills on time, keep credit card balances in check, and steer clear of unnecessary credit inquiries. It's like maintaining your impeccable style – consistency and attention to detail are key.

Regularly monitor your credit reports—it's akin to checking your outfit in a mirror before stepping out.

Detect and correct any errors promptly to ensure your financial attire remains impeccable. A flawless credit score is your secret weapon in the fashion-forward world of finance.

Your credit score is your financial accessory, so why not flaunt it like a fashion icon? Just as you'd showcase a statement necklace or a chic pair of sunglasses, your credit score is your ticket to financial elegance.

In conclusion, my fashionable financiers, managing debt is as much about style as it is about substance. Clear out those financial closets, prioritize high-interest debts, negotiate like a pro, and flaunt your credit score like a fabulous accessory. Debt management can be just as chic as updating your wardrobe for a new season, so embrace these sassy strategies and strut your stuff on the runway of financial success!

Chapter 6: Mindset Matters: Overcoming Financial Obstacles

Greetings, my glamorous financial connoisseurs. We're about to embark on a journey of the mind—where confidence, positivity, and resilience are the ultimate accessories that turn any financial ensemble into a showstopper. So, grab your metaphorical stilettos, and let's strut down the runway of financial success with unshakable style, grace, and a dash of humor.

Conquering Financial Fears: Strut Down the Runway of Life with Confidence!

Picture this, you're backstage at a fashion show, anxiously waiting to strut your stuff on the runway. Your heart races, and your knees wobble. This feeling isn't so different from the anxiety many of us feel when facing our financial fears. Financial fears can be daunting, but they shouldn't hold you back. It's time to conquer them with the same confidence that propels you down that runway!

Identify your financial fears—whether it's investing, budgeting, or facing debt—and confront them head-on. Take small steps to overcome these fears. Once you've pinpointed your fashion faux pas, tackle them head-on. Like a model learning to walk gracefully, educate yourself, seek guidance from experts, and remember that confidence is the ultimate accessory in the world of finance.

I remember my first time investing in the stock market. It felt like stepping onto that runway with all eyes on me. But I decided to conquer my financial fears, just as I'd conquer the runway, one small investment at a time.

Cultivating a Positive Money Mindset: Money as a Fabulous Accessory That Enhances Your Life!

Your money mindset is like your fashion sense—it shapes your choices and impacts your life. Think of money as a fabulous accessory that enhances your life's ensemble. Cultivating a positive money mindset is your key to financial elegance.

For me, shifting from a scarcity mindset to an abundance mindset was a game-changer. I began to view money not as a limited resource but as an abundant force in my life. Just as a fashionista sees endless style possibilities, I recognized that opportunities to grow my wealth were abundant.

Start by shifting your perspective. Visualize your financial goals with the same clarity as you would visualize your dream wardrobe. Embrace the concept of financial abundance. It's like adding that fabulous accessory that elevates your entire outfit. Your mindset will shape your financial journey just as your style shapes your overall presence.

Your money mindset is like your unique sense of style—it defines your choices and influences how you present yourself to the world. Think of money as the perfect accessory that enhances your life's ensemble.

Cultivating a positive money mindset is like finding that signature piece that complements your entire wardrobe.

Dealing with Setbacks: Bounce Back Like a Diva Who Stumbled in Her Stilettos!

Now, let's talk about setbacks—those financial stumbles that can feel as embarrassing as tripping on a runway in front of a packed audience. We've all been there, right? I certainly have.

In the world of finance, setbacks are like stumbling in your stilettos—they happen to the best of us. What sets you apart is how you bounce back. A true financial diva never lets a stumble define her journey.

I once made a not-so-glamorous investment that turned out to be a financial stumble. But I didn't let it define my journey. Instead, I approached it like a diva who had momentarily faltered in her stilettos. I quickly realigned by goals and changed course.

When faced with setbacks—whether it's an unexpected expense or an investment that didn't pan out—keep your composure. Evaluate the situation, learn from it, and adjust your financial strategies accordingly. Just as a diva gracefully recovers her stride on the runway, you can regain your financial footing with the poise of a seasoned runway model.

Remember, setbacks are part of the journey. Just as a diva owns her stumble and continues down the runway with confidence, you too can recover gracefully and continue strutting toward financial success.

Staying Motivated on Your Financial Journey: Keep Your Eye on the Prize!

Motivation is like the sparkly earrings that complete your stunning outfit—a small but essential detail that enhances your overall look. Maintaining motivation on your financial journey is akin to preparing for a glamorous event. It's all about keeping your eye on the prize—the fabulous life you're building. Like a celebrity getting ready for a red-carpet appearance, stay focused on your financial goals.

Setting clear, achievable milestones along the way is like planning your wardrobe for a series of red-carpet events. Celebrate your victories, whether they're as small as finding a great bargain or as monumental as paying off a significant debt. It's like acknowledging the compliments you receive for your impeccable style. Surround yourself with a supportive financial entourage. Your entourage is your backstage crew, your personal stylists who ensure you look your best. Surround yourself with friends, mentors, and financial advisers who will keep you motivated and on the right path just as celebrities have their teams of stylists and advisers. This network will keep you motivated and on track.

Lastly, remember that your financial journey is a marathon, not a sprint. As you make progress, visualize yourself achieving the ultimate goal—the financial freedom to live life on your terms. Like a starlet arriving at a glamorous event, you're destined for a grand entrance into the world of financial success.

Just as your style and confidence define your presence on the runway of life, your mindset shapes your financial success. Conquer your fears, cultivate a positive money mindset, bounce back from setbacks, and stay motivated with your eye on the prize. Financial success is your runway, and you're ready to own it with grace and style!

Chapter 7: Sassy Tips, Tricks, and Secrets for Saving and Budgeting

Today, we're about to embark on a journey of the mind—where confidence, positivity, and resilience are the ultimate accessories that turn any financial ensemble into a showstopper. So, grab your metaphorical stilettos, and let's strut down the runway of financial success with style, grace, and a dash of humor.

Budgeting with Style: Saving Money Is Like Finding a Designer Handbag on Sale!

Budgeting might sound about as exciting as watching paint dry, but trust me, it's like discovering that exquisite designer handbag you've been eyeing for months—only it's on sale! Budgeting with style is the key to unlocking your financial potential.

When I first started budgeting, I'll admit, it felt like trying to fit into a sample-size dress after a holiday feast—tight and uncomfortable. But once I got the hang of it, budgeting became my trusty sidekick, helping me manage my finances with flair.

To get started, examine your income and expenses, just like you'd review your wardrobe to curate outfits for different occasions. Create a budget that outlines your financial goals, from saving for a fabulous vacation to investing in a timeless piece of jewelry.

Budgeting is your fashion roadmap to achieving those financial fashion milestones!

Creating a Fabulous Budget: It's Like Planning a Wardrobe for Every Occasion!

Creating a budget is like planning your wardrobe for a year of fashion-forward events. You wouldn't wear the same outfit to a gala as you would to a casual brunch, right? Similarly, your budget should adapt to your financial goals and lifestyle.

Include all your sources of income and list your expenses with precision. Just as you'd choose the right outfit for a specific occasion, allocate your money wisely to different financial priorities. Whether it's setting aside funds for investing, building an emergency fund, or treating yourself to a little splurge, your budget is your stylist for life's financial runway.

Cutting Expenses Without Sacrificing Style: Look Fabulous on a Budget, Like a True Fashionista!

Now, let's talk about the art of cutting expenses without losing your fashion sense. It's all about looking fabulous on a budget, just like a true fashionista! Trust me; you don't need to sacrifice style to save money.

Start by scrutinizing your spending habits. Just as a fashionista reviews her wardrobe to identify what she no longer needs, comb through your expenses to spot areas where you can cut back. Maybe it's that daily designer coffee that can be swapped for a more affordable brew, or those impulse fashion purchases that can be curbed.

Remember, saving money is like finding a hidden gem in a thrift store—it's thrilling and oh-so-satisfying! Keep an eye out for deals, discounts, and cashback offers. Just as a fashion-savvy shopper knows how to hunt for bargains, you too can find ways to reduce expenses without compromising your signature style.

Building an Emergency Fund: Be Prepared for Unexpected Fashion Emergencies!

Ah, the emergency fund—a financial safety net that's as essential as having that go-to little black dress in your closet. Building an emergency fund is like being prepared for unexpected fashion emergencies. You never know when you might need it, but when you do, it's a lifesaver!

Life can throw curveballs at you, just as a last-minute fashion mishap can occur. Whether it's a sudden medical expense, a car repair, or even a fabulous fashion sale that's too good to resist, having an emergency fund provides the peace of mind to tackle these unexpected situations.

Start by setting aside a portion of your income regularly. Treat it like a fashion accessory fund—a little goes a long way. Aim to build up enough to cover three to six months' worth of living expenses. That way, when life throws you a financial curveball, you'll be ready to conquer it like a true fashionista.

The Art of Investing: Growing Your Wealth Like a Chic Investment Piece

Now that we've mastered budgeting and saving, let's talk about the exciting world of investing. Investing is like adding a timeless investment piece to your wardrobe—it grows in value and enhances your overall financial style.

I recall my first foray into investing; it felt like purchasing a coveted fashion item. I did my research, consulted experts, and carefully selected investments that aligned with my financial goals. Just as a fashionista invests in quality pieces that stand the test of time, I invested with an eye on long-term growth.

Consider various investment options, from stocks and bonds to real estate and mutual funds. Diversify your investment portfolio like a well-curated closet, spreading your risk while maximizing potential returns. And remember, just as fashion trends change, so do market conditions. Stay informed, adapt your investment strategy when needed, and watch your wealth grow like a fashion icon's collection.

Planning for Retirement: The Ultimate Wardrobe for Your Golden Years

As we continue our financial journey, let's not forget about retirement planning. Retirement is like having a wardrobe stocked with timeless classics, ensuring you're well-prepared for your golden years.

I've always believed in planning for retirement early, just as I invest in timeless fashion pieces that will always be in vogue. Whether you have access to a company-sponsored retirement plan or you're considering individual retirement accounts (IRAs), start saving for retirement as soon as possible.

Allocate a portion of your income to your retirement fund, just as you budget for your fashion purchases. Take advantage of employer contributions, if available, as it's like getting a discount on a coveted fashion item. And don't forget to regularly review and adjust your retirement strategy, ensuring it aligns with your evolving financial goals.

In conclusion, my fabulous readers, saving, budgeting, and investing are the cornerstones of your financial wardrobe. With these strategies, you can look fabulous on a budget, prepare for unexpected financial surprises, and build a solid financial foundation for your future. Just as a fashionista curates her wardrobe, curate your financial style with confidence and panache, and watch your financial success shine like the most coveted fashion statement on the runway of life!

Chapter 8: The Power of Investing in Yourself

Today, we're diving into a realm that's as essential as owning that perfect little black dress—the power of investing in yourself. Think of it as adorning yourself with valuable accessories that enhance your unique style and set you apart from the crowd.

Education and Personal Development: Invest in Your Knowledge!

Picture this, you're at a glitzy event, and you spot a statement necklace that you simply must have. Investing in yourself is like that necklace—it's the dazzling accessory that completes your financial ensemble.

Back when I decided to broaden my financial horizons, I went back to college at the age of 29 and focused on accounting, finance, and investing. It was like shopping for a limited edition handbag—I couldn't resist. The more I invested in my knowledge, the more I learned, the more confident I felt navigating the complex world of finance.

Education and personal development are like the exquisite accessories that complete your ensemble. They add depth, character, and uniqueness to your financial style. Just as you'd invest in a stunning piece of jewelry to elevate your look, investing in your knowledge and skills is a surefire way to elevate your financial game.

Consider furthering your education or acquiring new skills in areas that align with your passions and career goals. It's like adding a fabulous accessory to your skill set. Attend workshops, take courses, or pursue advanced degrees if it suits your aspirations. The more you invest in yourself, the more you enrich your financial palette and expand your opportunities.

I can't stress this enough—never underestimate the power of being a lifelong learner. Just as fashion evolves, so do industries and markets. Staying informed and continuously upgrading your skills is the key to remaining relevant in the ever-changing world of finance.

Building a Personal Brand: Showcase Your Uniqueness Like a Fashion-Forward Trendsetter!

Now, let's talk about building a personal brand. Think of it as defining your financial style, just like a fashion-forward trendsetter. After all, who wants to be a financial wallflower?

I once tried to blend in with the financial crowd, thinking that was the way to go. But then, I realized that blending in is about as fashionable as wearing socks with sandals. I decided to embrace my uniqueness as a Black woman in finance, showcase my strengths, and build a personal brand that reflected my fabulous self.

Don't be shy about highlighting your achievements and quirks. Just as fashion evolves, so does your personal brand. Keep it fresh, exciting, and authentic. After all, you're the trendsetter of your financial journey, and your brand should be as unique as your favorite couture piece.

In the digital age, building a personal brand is like creating a signature fashion style that defines who you are. It's about showcasing your uniqueness like a fashion-forward trendsetter. Start by identifying your strengths, values, and passions. Create a personal brand that reflects your essence. Share your expertise, thoughts, and experiences through blogs, social media, or even public speaking. Your personal brand is your fashion statement in the world of finance—it should leave a memorable impression.

Networking Like a Pro: Make Connections That Sparkle, Just Like Your Favorite Statement Necklace!

Networking is like having a collection of statement necklaces in your closet. Each connection adds a bit of sparkle to your financial journey, just like an eye-catching accessory. Attending industry events, joining professional groups, and seeking out mentors are all like the fashion show of the financial world. It's where you can exchange ideas, learn from others, and, if you're lucky, find your financial soulmate—er, I mean, business partner.

I once attended a financial networking event with a pocketful of business cards, thinking I'd make a dazzling impression. But, let's just say I ended up looking like I was playing a game of financial poker. I quickly learned that networking isn't about collecting cards; it's about forming genuine connections.

Remember, just as your statement necklace complements your outfit, your network should complement your goals. Nurture these relationships, offer support, and be genuinely interested in others. Building a network of valuable connections is like having a treasure chest of dazzling accessories to choose from when the financial occasion calls for it.

Taking Care of Your Physical and Mental Well-Being: Prioritize Self-Care Like a True Queen!

Lastly, let's talk about the most important accessory of all—yourself! Your physical and mental well-being is like the crown that adorns a queen. Without it, nothing else in your financial wardrobe will shine.

I once thought I could conquer the financial world by burning the candle at both ends. But guess what happened? I ended up resembling a sleep-deprived zombie who'd lost her sense of humor. That's when I realized that self-care isn't a luxury—it's a necessity.

Prioritize self-care, just as a queen cherishes her well-being. Maintain a healthy lifestyle through exercise, nutrition, and regular check-ups. Your body is like a designer outfit—it deserves to be treated with care and respect.

Don't forget about your mental well-being, either. Seek balance, manage stress, and practice mindfulness. Your mind is like a treasure chest of creativity and resilience—keep it sharp and polished. Consider meditation, therapy, or simply engaging in activities that bring you joy, like indulging in your favorite fashion purchases.

In conclusion, my fabulous readers, investing in yourself is the ultimate financial fashion statement. Just as fashion enthusiasts invest in timeless pieces, invest in your knowledge, personal brand, network, and well-being. Build a personal brand that screams "you," network like a pro, and prioritize self-care. These investments will enrich your financial journey, make you stand out like a trendsetter, and ensure you shine like the true queen of your financial realm. After all, you are your most valuable asset in the world of finance, and it's time to shine like the brightest diamond in the jewelry store!

Chapter 9: Celebrating Milestones and Enjoying the Fruits of Your Labor

It's time to roll out the metaphorical red carpet, pop the champagne, and dance like nobody's watching because we're about to explore the art of celebrating financial milestones with all the glitz, glam, and sass you can imagine!

Pop the Champagne and Dance Like Nobody's Watching: Celebrating Your Financial Wins!

Imagine this: you've just achieved a major financial milestone, and it feels like stumbling upon that designer dress you've been lusting after at a sample sale. What's the first thing you do? You pop the champagne and dance like nobody's watching! Celebrating your financial victories is like adding the most exquisite accessory to your ensemble—it elevates your confidence and makes you feel on top of the world.

I recall a moment when my investments finally paid off. It was like strutting down a glittering runway, bathed in the spotlight of success. So, my financial divas, whether it's paying off a mountain of debt, reaching a savings goal that seemed unattainable, or smashing a career milestone, never forget to celebrate. Throw a fabulous soirée, treat yourself to a special indulgence, or simply revel in the joy of your achievements. Life's too short not to pop a few corks and dance the night away!

Now, let's dive into the delightful world of rewarding yourself. Treating yourself is like embarking on a decadent shopping spree, but instead of buying material possessions, you're investing in priceless experiences that money can't buy.

After reaching any significant financial goal such as when my investment portfolio on Robinhood hit $100,000, I decided to treat myself to a luxurious spa day at the Ritz Carlton. I spent 6 hours at the spa getting body wraps, massages, and a facial. It was like slipping into the softest cashmere sweater—a true indulgence for the soul. Treating yourself to fabulous experiences is like adding the most precious gem to your collection of memories.

Whether it's a weekend getaway to a picturesque destination, a gourmet dining experience that tantalizes your taste buds, or a day of pampering at the spa, remember that you've earned it. Just as a fashionista deserves to indulge in luxury now and then, you deserve to savor the sweet taste of success. So, go ahead, reward yourself, and create unforgettable memories along your financial journey.

Giving Back to the Community: Share Your
Success and Uplift Others Like a True
Philanthropist!

As we raise our glasses to toast our financial milestones, let's not forget the importance of giving back. Sharing your success and uplifting others is like donating your most cherished fashion pieces to those in need—it's an act of kindness that never goes out of style.

When I reached a certain level of financial stability, I decided to start a scholarship program for underprivileged students entering the field of accounting. I donated $5,000 per year for these deserving high school students. It felt like creating a fashion line that not only makes people look good but also does good for the community. Giving back is like the ultimate fashion statement—it showcases your generosity and compassion and is more rewarding than shopping at Louis Vuitton.

Consider donating to causes close to your heart, volunteering your time and skills, or even starting your charitable initiatives. Just as fashion trends change with the seasons, so do the needs of our communities. Be a philanthropic trendsetter and make a difference in the lives of others. Remember, the joy of giving is like the perfect pair of shoes—it always fits just right.

Balancing Financial Success and Happiness: Create a Life That Fits You Perfectly!

Lastly, let's discuss the delicate balance between financial success and happiness. It's like finding the perfect outfit—every piece should fit you perfectly.

I used to chase financial success at the expense of my happiness. I worked tireless hours and barely saw my family. It left me feeling like I was wearing a pair of shoes that pinched my toes and I couldn't find anywhere to sit down. I quickly realized that no amount of wealth is worth sacrificing your joy and well-being.

Create a life that fits you perfectly. Balance your financial goals with your passions and desires. It's like curating a wardrobe that's uniquely you—every piece should make you feel confident, comfortable, and joyful. Remember financial success isn't the end-all-be-all; it's a tool that should enhance your life, not define it. Just as fashion trends evolve, so do your priorities and dreams. Adjust your financial journey to align with your happiness, and you'll discover that the perfect fit is the key to a fulfilling life.

Celebrating your financial milestones is a must in this fabulous journey. Pop the champagne, reward yourself with unforgettable experiences, give back to your community, and find the balance between financial success and happiness. Life is too short not to enjoy the fruits of your labor with style and grace. So, go out there and shine like the stars you are on the runway of life!

Chapter 10: Sassy Investor for Generations to Come: Legacy Planning

Welcome to the grand finale where we embark on a journey into the intricate world of legacy planning. In this chapter, we will delve into the art of creating a lasting financial legacy, imparting financial wisdom to future generations, engaging in charitable endeavors, and meticulously planning for retirement. Think of it as the masterstroke that puts the final flourish on your financial canvas.

Leaving a Lasting Financial Legacy: Passing Down a Collection of Timeless Fashion Pieces!

Consider this scenario: you've diligently accumulated wealth, built a thriving empire, and now it's time to ponder the legacy you'll leave behind. Legacy planning is akin to assembling a collection of timeless fashion pieces, carefully chosen to transcend generations—a legacy that continues to enrich lives even after you're gone.

Legacy planning is your opportunity to ensure your hard-earned wealth benefits your loved ones and future generations, much like a prized fashion item that never goes out of style. Consider estate planning, wills, and trusts as tools to preserve and protect your assets. But remember, a legacy is not just about money; it's about values, wisdom, and principles. Just as a fashionista invests in timeless pieces that stand the test of time, invest in your legacy to make an enduring impact on your loved ones and beyond.

Teaching Financial Literacy to Future Generations: Empower Your Loved Ones with Knowledge!

Let's explore the pivotal role of teaching financial literacy to future generations. Think of it as passing down the secrets to creating a signature style that will stand the test of time. Teaching financial literacy is about empowering your loved ones with the knowledge and skills they need to navigate their financial journeys with confidence.

Consider providing financial education, mentoring, and guidance to your family members. Equip them with the tools to make informed decisions about investing, budgeting, and managing their finances. Just as a seasoned fashionista imparts style tips to the next generation, share your financial insights to ensure your legacy thrives through generations.

Charitable Giving: Make a Difference in the World Like a True Style Icon!

Charitable giving is the art of adding a philanthropic touch to your financial legacy—a way of making a profound impact on the world, much like a style icon inspires and influences. Charitable giving allows you to leverage your financial success to uplift those in need and leave an indelible mark on society.

Consider establishing a foundation, supporting causes that align with your values, or contributing to organizations that resonate with your passions. Just as a fashion icon uses their platform to inspire and influence, your charitable giving can ignite positive change in the world.

Planning for Retirement: Enjoy Your Golden Years in Style

Lastly, let's delve into the meticulous planning for retirement. Retirement is akin to savoring your golden years in style, the grand finale of your financial journey. Deliberate retirement planning involves diligent saving, exploring various retirement accounts, and consulting with financial experts to craft a retirement plan as tailored as your favorite bespoke suit or elegant dress. Retirement is your time to shine, to revel in the experiences you've worked diligently for, and to luxuriate in the fruits of your labor with grace and style.

In conclusion, legacy planning is the pièce de résistance, the final brushstroke on your financial canvas. Whether you're crafting a lasting financial legacy, imparting financial wisdom to future generations, engaging in charitable endeavors, or meticulously planning for retirement, do so with the gravitas, elegance, and wisdom befitting a true financial maestro. As we bid adieu to our journey, remember that your legacy is not confined to wealth; it encompasses the values and impact you leave behind in the world. Go forth and shine like the diva you are, and may your financial legacy stand as a beacon for generations to come.

www.ingramcontent.com/pod-product-compliance
Lightning Source LLC
Chambersburg PA
CBHW080112010626
45794CB00016B/3694